|NDIGO

T0273400

Also by Ellen Bass

Poetry

Like a Beggar

The Human Line

Mules of Love

No More Masks! An Anthology of Poems by Women,
coedited with Florence Howe

Nonfiction

*Free Your Mind: The Book for Gay, Lesbian, and Bisexual Youth—
and Their Allies,* coauthored with Kate Kaufman

*Beginning to Heal: A First Book for Men and Women
Who Were Sexually Abused as Children,*
coauthored with Laura Davis

The Courage to Heal: A Guide for Women Survivors of Child Sexual Abuse,
coauthored with Laura Davis

I Never Told Anyone: Writings by Women Survivors of Child Sexual Abuse,
coedited with Louise Thornton and others

INDIGO

ELLEN BASS

COPPER CANYON PRESS

PORT TOWNSEND, WASHINGTON

Cover art: Photograph of Paul Snooks, tattoo by Phill Bonds. From *The Art of the Tattoo* by Henry Ferguson and Lynn Procter (Courage Books, 1998).

Copper Canyon Press is in residence at Fort Worden State Park in Port Townsend, Washington, under the auspices of Centrum. Centrum is a gathering place for artists and creative thinkers from around the world, students of all ages and backgrounds, and audiences seeking extraordinary cultural enrichment.

LIBRARY OF CONGRESS CATALOGING-IN-PUBLICATION DATA
Names: Bass, Ellen, author.
Title: Indigo / Ellen Bass.
Description: Port Townsend : Copper Canyon Press, [2020] |
Identifiers: LCCN 2019043838 | ISBN 9781556595752 (trade paperback)
Classification: LCC PS3552.A817 I53 2020 | DDC 811/.54—dc23
LC record available at https://lccn.loc.gov/2019043838

9 8 7 6 5 4 3 2

COPPER CANYON PRESS
Post Office Box 271
Port Townsend, Washington 98368
www.coppercanyonpress.org

Acknowledgments

Grateful acknowledgment is made to the following publications in which these poems or earlier versions first appeared (sometimes with different titles):

Academy of American Poets Poem-a-Day: "Any Common Desolation," "Enough," "Fungus on Fallen Alder at Lookout Creek," "Sink Your Fingers into the Darkness of My Fur"

The American Poetry Review: "Goat, Cow, Man," "Grizzly," "The Kitchen Counter," "On My Father's Illness," "Pushing," "Sometimes I'm frightened," "Taking Off the Front of the House"

Catamaran: "Experiment in Empathy"

The Comstock Review: "Sometimes, when she is buried deep"

Five Points: "Ode to the Pork Chop"

Kenyon Review: "Pines at Ponary"

Narrative: "Because What We Do Does Not Die," "How It Began," "Listening," "The Long Recovery," "Ode to Zeke," "Wilderness"

New Voices: Contemporary Writers Confronting the Holocaust: "Photograph: Jews Probably Arriving to the Lodz Ghetto circa 1941–1942"

The New Yorker: "After Long Illness," "Because," "Blame," "Failure," "Indigo," "The Orange-and-White High-Heeled Shoes," "Reincarnation," "The Small Country"

Orion: "Bringing Flowers to Salinas Valley State Prison," "Roses"

Ploughshares: "I look over and there she is"

Plume: "Gopher"

Poet Lore: "Not Dead Yet"

Poetry: "I Could Touch It," "Marriage"

Poetry International: "Mammogram Callback with Ultrasound," "Sous-Chef"

Rattle: "Black Coffee"

The Sun: "Getting into Bed on a December Night," "Kiss," "Ode to Fat," "Taking My Old Dog Out to Pee before Bed"

Terminus Magazine: "Pearls"

"Any Common Desolation" was included in the 2017 *Pushcart Prize XLI: Best of the Small Presses.*

Gratitude to the National Endowment for the Arts and to the Andrews Forest Long-Term Ecological Reflections Writers-in-Residence Program.

Thank you to my three essential mentors who made this life of poetry possible for me: Florence Howe, Anne Sexton, and Dorianne Laux. For generous and insightful comments on these poems, thank you to Jericho Brown, Janet Bryer, Toi Derricotte, Marie Howe, Danusha Laméris, Clare Wesley, Cynthia White, and, most especially, Frank X. Gaspar. My gratitude to Michael Wiegers, editor extraordinaire, to Joseph Bednarik, George Knotek, and everyone at Copper Canyon Press for your dedication to poetry. Thank you to my agent, Charlotte Raymond, for your loyalty and encouragement over four decades. Thank you to my students for being my teachers. Thank you to my best friend, Beverly Sky, for schlepping around the world with me for fifty years. Thank you to Lesley and Michael Tierra for your kindness. Thank you, Sophie Bryer, my sister-out-law, for your support. Thank you to my daughter, Swati, for your generosity. And to Janet, my love, for all of it.

For Max

Tell me a story.

In this century, and moment, of mania,
Tell me a story.

Make it a story of great distances, and starlight.

The name of the story will be Time,
But you must not pronounce its name.

ROBERT PENN WARREN

Contents

INDIGO

Sous-Chef

I like cutting the cucumber, the knife slicing the darkness
into almost-transparent moons, each
with its own thin rim of night. I like smashing
the garlic with the flat of steel
and peeling the sticky, papery skin from the clove.
Tell me what to do. I'm free of will.
I carve the lamb into one-inch cubes.
I don't use a ruler, but I'd be happy to.
Give me a tomato bright as a parrot.
Give me peaches like burning clouds.
I'll pare those globes until dawn. The syrup
will linger on my fingers like your scent.
Let me escape my own insistence.
I am the bee feeding the queen.
Show me how you want
the tart glazed. I still have opinions,
but I don't believe in them.
Let me fillet the supple bones from the fish.
Let me pit the cherries. Husk the corn.
You say how much cinnamon
to spice the stew. I've made bad decisions,
so I'm grateful for this yoke
lowered onto my shoulders, potatoes
mounded before me.
With all that's destroyed, look
how the world still yields a golden pear.
Freckled and floral, a shimmering marvel.
It rests in my palm so heavily, perfectly.
Somewhere there is hunger. Somewhere, fear.
But here the chopping block is solid. My blade sharp.

The Small Country

Unique, I think, is the Scottish *tartle*, that hesitation
when introducing someone whose name you've forgotten

and what could capture *cafuné*, the Brazilian Portuguese way to say
running your fingers, tenderly, through someone's hair?

Is there a term in any tongue for choosing to be happy?

And where is speech for the block of ice we pack in the sawdust of our hearts?

What appellation approaches the smell of apricots thickening the air
when you boil jam in early summer?

What words reach the way I touched you last night—
as though I had never known a woman—an explorer,
wholly curious to discover each particular
fold and hollow, without guide,
not even the mirror of my own body.

Last night you told me you liked my eyebrows.
You said you never really noticed them before.
What is the word that fuses this freshness
with the pity of having missed it.

And how even touch itself cannot mean the same to both of us,
even in this small country of our bed,
even in this language with only two native speakers.

Reincarnation

Who would believe in reincarnation
if she thought she would return as
an oyster? Eagles and wolves
are popular. Even domesticated cats
have their appeal. It's not terribly distressing
to imagine being Missy, nibbling
kibble and lounging on the windowsill.
But I doubt the toothsome oyster has ever
been the totem of any shaman
fanning the Motherpeace Tarot
or smudging with sage.
Yet perhaps we could do worse
than aspire to be a plump bivalve. Humbly,
the oyster persists in filtering
seawater and fashioning the daily
irritations into luster.
Dash a dot of Tabasco, pair it
with a dry martini, not only
will this tender button inspire
an erotic fire in tuxedoed men
and women whose shoulders gleam
in candlelight, this hermit praying
in its rocky cave, this anchorite of iron,
calcium, and protein, is practically
a molluscan saint. Revered and sacrificed,
body and salty liquor of the soul,
the oyster is devoured, surrendering
all—again and again.

The Orange-and-White High-Heeled Shoes

Today I'm thinking about those shoes—white
with a tangerine stripe across the toe and forceful orange heels—

that fit both my mother and me. We used to shop like that—
trying them on side by side. That was when there still

was a man who would cradle your heel in his palm
and guide your foot. Sometimes he would think he made a sale,

only to have one of us turn to the other—
and he would have to kneel again, hoping to ease another naked sole

into the bed of suede or leather. I thought those shoes
were just the peak of chic. And—my God—

she bought me a pair of orange cotton gloves to complete the ensemble.
Why is there such keen pleasure in remembering?

You are dead ten years. And these showy slippers—
we wore them more than half a century ago. The first boy

had not yet misted my breasts with his breath
and you were strong as a muscled goddess, gliding nylons

over your calves, lifting your amplitude into a breastplate.
Who will remember these pumpkin-colored pumps

when I die, too? Who will remember how we slid into them
like girls diving into a cedar-tinged lake, like bees

entering the trumpet of a flower, like birds disappearing
into the green, green leaves of summer?

Taking Off the Front of the House

I'm at the kitchen table, drinking strong tea, eating eggs
with poppy-gold yolks from our chickens, Marilyn and Estelle.
There's a red car parked across the street and my neighbor's gorgeous irises,
their frilled tongues tasting the air.
"Monsanto is suing Vermont," I say, turning the pages of the *Times*.
I say it loud because Janet's in the living room
in the faded chair the cat has scratched into hay
eating yogurt and the strawberries she brought home from the field
where she labors to relieve the tender berry of its heavy chemical load.
"What?" she says. She isn't wearing her hearing aids
so I take a breath and project my voice. And as I enunciate the corporate evils,
suddenly the front of the house is sheared away.
We're on a stage, the audience seated on the asphalt of Younglove Avenue,
watching this quirky couple eat their breakfast and yell
back and forth from one room to another.
And throughout the day, as I throw a load of laundry
in the dryer, answer the phone, as she lies on the couch
reading *Great Expectations* and we bicker
about the knocking in the pipes and whether we really need to call a plumber,
I admire how the actor who plays the character of me
and the actor who plays the character of her
perform our parts so perfectly
in this production that will last
just a little while before it closes for good.
And when night comes, we smoke a little weed—something called
        Thunder Fuck,
which must be someone's high opinion of himself,
but in truth is quite nice, though we only take a couple tokes
since Janet's on blood pressure medication and she can't
do the way she did at twenty when she slung a goatskin bag
over her shoulder and wandered around Senegal in flip-flops.
As I reach for her, she says, "Now the audience can sit on the back deck
by the barbecue and this play can be called
The Old Lesbians Go to Bed at the End of the Day."

I light the candle her mother gave me for my last birthday
when she could still put on her lipstick.
The set is authentic—a messy stack of books on my nightstand,
on her side, the hearing aids that sit there all day.
And as she turns toward me and I feel again
the marvelous architecture of her hips, the moon,
that expert in lighting, rises over the roofline,
flooding us in her flawless silvery wash.

Ode to the Pork Chop

As oil blisters in the cast-iron pan, my dog does
adoring prostrations at my feet and the pale pink chops
with their arc of rib and ribbon of fat lie innocently
on the white bone china we bought at Macy's
where my wife asked the salesclerk what kind of bones
the dishes were made from and the woman confessed
she had no idea, though surely they were crushed
from sorrowful creatures. Everything you do will cause
harm, so I start forgiving myself now. And this pig
was a happy pig, and his death, though death,
was good. I've boiled up his vertebrae, femurs
and fibulae, his head and his hocks,
and now the stock is cooling, the creamy lard rising
to the top like a thick slab of heaven. When these
choice cuts hit the skillet, the hiss and spit is
a lullaby that's soothed homo sapiens
since the discovery of fire. And lured the dogs
into the circle, shoulders hunched toward the flames.
As meat sears and butter bubbles, that sizzling
tells us all will be well. The egg will be released
from the ovary, the swaddled infant will suck.
There will be mayhem and there will be bliss,
and stuffed into every cell of our bodies,
that deep craving for grease.

Enough

Enough seen . . . Enough had . . . Enough . . .
ARTHUR RIMBAUD

No. It will never be enough. Never
enough wind clamoring in the trees,
sun and shadow handling each leaf, never enough clang
of my neighbor hammering,
the iron nails, relenting wood, sound waves
lapping over roofs, never enough
bees purposeful at the throats
of lilies. How could we be replete
with the flesh of ripe tomatoes, the crushed
scent of their leaves? It would take many
births to be done with the thatness of that.

Oh, blame life. That we just want more.
Summer rain. Mud. A cup of tea.
Our teeth, our eyes. A baby in a stroller.
Another spoonful of crème brûlée,
sweet burnt crust crackling.
And hot showers, oh lovely, lovely hot showers.

Today was a good day.
My mother-in-law sat on the porch, eating crackers and cheese
with a watered-down margarita
and though her nails are no longer stoplight red
and she can't remember who's alive or dead,
still, this was a day
with no unstoppable weeping.

Last night, through the small window of my laptop,
I watched a dying man kill himself in Switzerland.
He wore a blue shirt and snow was falling
onto a small blue house, onto dark needles of pine and fir.
He didn't step outside to feel the snow on his face.
He sat at a table with his wife and drank poison.

Online I found a plastic bag complete with Velcro
and a hole for a tube to a propane tank. I wouldn't have to
move our Weber. I could just slide
down the stucco to the flagstones, where healthy
weeds are sprouting through the cracks.
Maybe it wouldn't be half bad
to go out looking at the yellowing leaves of the old camellia.
And from there I could see the chickens scratching—
if we still have chickens then. And yet . . .

this little hat of life, how will I bear
to take it off while I can still reach up? Snug woolen watch cap,
lacy bonnet, yellow cloche with the yellow veil
I wore the Easter I turned thirteen when my mother let me
            promenade
with Tommy Spagnola on the boardwalk in Atlantic City.

Oxygen, oxygen, the cry of the body—
but there may come a day
when I must say *no—*
enough, enough
with more tenderness
than I have ever given to a lover, the gift
of the nipple hardening under my fingertip, more
tenderness than to my newborn,
when I held her still streaked
with my blood. I'll say the most gentle refusal
to this dear animal and tighten
the clasp around my throat that once was kissed and kissed
until the blood could no longer rest in its channel, but rose
to the surface like a fish that couldn't wait to be caught.

Sometimes I'm frightened

by how much I need her. It's raining this morning.
That hopeful sounding on the roof.

I can almost hear the roots
suck water through their fragile hairs,

raising it through the tough trunk
into the cloud-shaped canopy of the live oak

and all the sweet bright blades that startle up overnight.
When she recedes I feel how ragged I am.

The clouds are torn into bits. Each separate drop that falls
like a moment of needing her.

I can kiss her. I just can't keep on
kissing and kissing her. Even though

that's what I want. To fall
asleep with her lip between my teeth.

Sometimes I can taste the distance between us. Rain
trembles on the camellia's waxy leaves and spills

bead by bead from the tips. I can remember
being a child, opening my mouth to the rain.

Bringing Flowers to Salinas Valley State Prison

When Mr. H. saw the little meadow blooming
on the steel table, he bowed to the starry faces of jasmine.
This is the first flower I've smelled in twenty years.
And when I slid each man a bouquet in a paper cup
Mr. M. said, *I'll have such a short time with these.*
We spoke, then, about Beauty and Loss,
the great themes of poetry.
And when our time was done,
and the guard said they had to leave the flowers,
most of the men acquiesced. But Mr. S.
insisted he had, as a Native American, a right
to his rituals—sage, sweet corn, tobacco—
and no one could stop him—it was the law—
from taking these sacred plants back to his cell.
Then he raised his cup and drank
the water the flowers were drinking
and a small wind stirred in that windowless room
as we watched Mr. S. quietly bite
the heads off the Peruvian lilies,
crushing their pink sepals and the gold
inner petals flecked with maroon, swallowing
the silvery filaments, their dark
pollen-laden anthers, his mouth frothing with blossoms.

Taking My Old Dog Out to Pee before Bed

Zeke's hips are too ground down
to lift a leg, so he just stands there. We both
just stand, looking into the darkness.
The moon silvers his thinning fur.
Orion strides across the heavens, his own dog
trotting at his heel. And a great live oak reaches over
from the neighbor's yard, dense black limbs
silhouetted against a paler sky. Single voluptuous
remnant of forests. Can a tree be lonely?
Zeke tips up his muzzle, scent streaming
through two hundred million olfactory cells
as he reads the illuminated manuscript of night—
raccoons prowling down the street, who's in heat
or just out for a stroll. Handsome still,
he reminds me of an aging movie star with his striking
white eyebrows and square jaw. He always
had an urbane elegance, a gentleman
who could carry off satin lapels and a silver-tipped cane.
Tonight an ambulance wails. Someone not so far away
is frightened, in pain, trying to live or trying to die.
And then it's quiet again. No birds. No wind.
We don't speak. We just wait, alive together,
until one of us turns back to the door
and the other follows.

Getting into Bed on a December Night

When I slip beneath the quilt and fold into
her warmth, I think we are like the pages
of a love letter written thirty years ago
that some aging god still reads each day
and then tucks back into its envelope.

How It Began

She called. Her voice was naked
with fear. Before that, there were signs,
but we didn't know they were signs.
I was sitting on a blue couch
a few hundred miles from home.
I held a cup of tea. She told me
she'd jolted awake with her heart stampeding.
No, she would have said *pounding*. Or maybe
racing. What people say. I knew
how to help her breathe. I breathed
with her, deep slow inhale and
long, longer exhale. I focused on that.
Oh honey, I said, *you don't want*
to go there. Let's turn this around.
But I've always believed too much
in my own will. I knew.
And didn't know.
Or didn't want to know I knew.
Though we both could feel the floor's slight pitch.
We were in for a long long voyage
without a chance to grab even
an orange or comb our hair.

Black Coffee

I didn't know that when my mother died, her grave
would be dug in my body. And when I weaken,
she is here, dressing behind the closet door,
hooking up her long-line cotton bra,
then sliding the cups around to the front,
leaning over and harnessing each heavy breast,
setting the straps in the grooves on her shoulders,
reins for the journey. She's slicking her lips with
Fire & Ice. She's shoveling the car out of the snow.
How many pints of Four Roses did she slide
into exactly sized brown bags? How many cases
of Pabst Blue Ribbon did she sling onto the counter?
All the crumpled bills, steeped in the smells
of the lives who'd handled them—their sweat,
onions and grease, lumber and bleach—she opened
her palm and smoothed each one. Then
stacked them precisely, restoring order.
And at ten, after the change fund was counted,
the doors locked, she uncinched the girth, unbuckled
the bridle. She cooked Cream of Wheat for my father,
mixed a milkshake with Hershey's syrup for me,
and poured herself a single highball,
placed on a yellow paper napkin.
Years later, when I needed the nightly
highball too, she gave me this story.
She'd left my father in the hospital—
this time they didn't know if he'd live,
but she had to get back to the store. Halfway,
she stopped at a diner and ordered coffee.
She sat in the booth with her coat still on,
crying, silently, just the tears rolling down,
and the waitress never said a word,
just kept refilling her cup.

The Long Recovery

When she would come home
from the strawberry fields, I'd empty
the dirt from the cuffs of her jeans,
scrub the mud ground into the knees.
It made me want to tongue the sweat
of her throat, taste salt
in the dusty crevices. No, no,
I say now to my dumb sex,
that like a dog can't understand.
I know I'm less than a speck on the planet,
the planet less than a speck
and so on. Is it sacred
or insane that I matter so much
to myself, that she
matters so much to me? What use
is my turning her again and again
toward the sun? I'm old
enough to know there's nothing
we love without incurring
the debt of grief. The maple leaves
just edged with crimson. The bright
yellow breast of the warbler, its
swee swee sweetie cry.
Her hand, as she lifts a cup, riddled
with veins, ruched, the loose
skin almost transparent, almost familiar
as my own. How can I hurl myself deeper
into this life? Why
do I think there's something better
I could be doing?
I miss her. I miss her. I believe
in her animal scent. I believe stars

burn in the blank day sky.
I believe the earth rushes through space
though I can't feel the slightest breeze.

Failure

I looked like a woman. I'd begun
to bleed, something I'd wanted with a fervor,
like the fervor with which I burned
to kiss Earl Freeman, to smell his man sweat
and finger the hollow at his breastbone
when we lay in the hot sand in Atlantic City,
the white sky arched over us. I was in such a hurry
to grow up, my mother said. But I was innocent
in the sense of not yet guilty
as I lifted the spoonful of oatmeal
to my father's lips
the day he came home from the hospital.
My mother had to go back to work—
Hy-Grade Wines and Liquors,
which paid for the brown Formica table and pink
refrigerator, pink dishwasher. We'd moved
from the apartment over the store
into a house with a front door.
I wanted people to ring the bell
and I'd answer it like on TV.
It didn't seem like it would be too hard
to feed my father. I can do it,
I assured my mother.
I think I may see us there forever, my weak father
in pajamas, me holding
the spoon of thin oatmeal, lifting it
to his lips and the lips not
taking it, not really willing or
unwilling. So the gruel
slid back out again, dribbling
down his badly shaved chin.
He did nothing to stop it. My father.
I left him there. This was my first

entrance into the land of failure, a country
I would visit so often
it would begin to feel like home.

Goat, Cow, Man

After the mob murdered the man for eating
a cow, it was found to be meat
from a goat. Why can I not
stop thinking about it—
the stringy flesh inside his gut,
and the microbes run riot when his heart
stopped—how fast they started
breaking down the blood-clotted
muscle of his stomach, slick intestines,
as though they were meant
to destroy the evidence of human—what
can I call it? sin? the curse of certainty? some twist
in the helix that insists on splitting
us apart?—the cow is not the goat. I am not
you. The man is a few inches of old newsprint,
a knot of hair, eye sockets,
but I keep picturing that
kitchen, his wife and children stuttering,
it's goat, it's goat,
and the goat, her white
coat, the little kernels of her teeth,
her pale slitted eyes.

Listening

What if geese honking overhead told you what it's like to travel so far?

Or a fish described the pierce of the hook, the shock of the line?

What if a leaf could whisper the slow ache
as the green drained away? Or a tree, the sudden ax?

What if we could hear *the small gnats mourn?*

Because

Because the night I gave birth my husband went blind.
Hysterical, I guess you'd call it.

Because there'd been too many people
and then there was no one. Only

this small creature—her tiny cry
no bigger than a sequin.

Because I'd been pushing too many hours.
Even with her soft skull plates shifting,

the collar of my bones too slender.
When I reached down

I could feel the wet wisps of hair of this being living
inside me, but her heart was weakening.

The midwife told me not to push
on the way to the hospital, but I pushed anyway.

This was California in the seventies and I'd have pushed
        until I died.
The doctor asked for permission to cut

my perineum. So polite, as though he were requesting
the pleasure of the next dance. Then he slid in forceps

skillfully, not a scratch on her temples.
But we left that haven the same night because my husband

didn't believe in hospitals, the baby naked,
wrapped only in a blanket because we both believed

in skin to skin. Because the baby cried
but wouldn't suck.

Because when I started to stand
I started to faint so I had to crawl

to the sterile diapers and pale yellow sleeper
folded inside the brown paper bag I'd baked in the oven.

Because I'm still there on my hands and knees,
deflated belly and ripe breasts, huge dark nipples,

tearing open the stapled bag,
fumbling the ducky pins,

two fingers slipped between the baby's belly
and the thick layers of cotton, the sharp point.

The baby, a stranger,
yet so strangely familiar,

flecks of blood still stuck to her scalp.
Because my husband slept

beside me and I let him sleep.
Because it would be years before I left him.

Now love and grief would be greater
than I ever imagined,

rooted together like north and south,
over and under.

Because I too had been pushed out
into another world

I lay there with the baby whimpering in my arms,
both of us wide awake in the darkness.

Wilderness

Break me like bread. Take me
apart. Strip each rib down to light.
Pour me out like a bucket of milk, sloshing
hot from the teats of a goat. Shear
my hair and toss it onto the back
of the wind for the birds to weave. As the egret
pecks at the elephant's hide,
as the plover scrapes the crocodile's teeth,
pick me clean. Whisper
to my lonely breasts. Tell them a story,
you are going to die. But don't let me go
until my body is a wilderness.
You be the whale. I, the krill.
Open your jaw and swim through my shoal.
Empty me like a cargo ship. Hoist
cases of whiskey and all the flaming
threads of saffron. Don't be patient.
Plunge your hand through my flesh
and pull out the nest of hair and teeth. Give me
eighteen sinuous arms like Avalokiteshvara
so I can hold you through every terror.
Give me infinite legs like the *Nude Descending*
so I can be always rushing toward you.

Experiment in Empathy

The scientist places each rat
in its own glass box
and for thirty seconds he plays
"What a Wonderful World."
In the last three seconds, he shocks the rat.
This is followed by ninety beats of silence.
And then the cycle begins again.

As she describes it to me
I can't help thinking
how familiar this is—one minute
Louis Armstrong singing
and the next—
some fever or wreck, some impossible mistake.
And I sit holding a spoon,
unable to lift it to my mouth, unable
to put it down.

This strain of rats descends
from a circus in the 1800s. Their ancestors
swung on satin-ribboned trapezes
and leaped through tiny rings of fire.
Now, none of those skills can save them.

And here's the thing:
a rat who isn't shocked,
who only watches,
panics too. That is empathy.
Feeling what another creature feels.

But sometimes it's too much to ask
a person to inhabit
the strange region of a foreign heart.

Once, when I was in a glut of pain,
I said to a friend,
Just take an hour and imagine
this is happening to you.

She looked straight ahead
and said, *I don't want to.*

Pearls

I'm sorry I didn't buy my father the cashmere sweater with suede trim
          the summer
I went to Europe. And I'm sorry I didn't stay longer with my mother after
          he died.

Why was I in such a hurry to get back to my husband who I only fought
          with anyway?
I'm sorry I kissed his best friend and came home smelling of wood
          smoke and sweat.

I'm sorry for the polar bears. And the whales. I once sailed so close
          I could hear
their breath, see the white scars etched into their flukes.

I read about a man who owns every clock in the opening sequence of
          Back to the Future.
And a man who collects dipsticks from old cars. I know I've hurt you.

I know you think I'm like them and you are one of my assemblages.
I know you think I have secret motives sewn like pearls into the hem of
          my coat.

You wake every morning surprised to feel your blood still making
          its rounds.
But I could die before you. You might be standing in your blooming yard

after a spring rain when your cell rings and someone you don't love
half as much as me tells you I'm gone. Oh my operas! My matinees!

But isn't this what some souls slit their exquisite wrists for?
A thousand torch songs crying out, an exaltation of larks.

Death is poorly camouflaged this morning. Ants are floating
in the broth of sugar and borax I mix for them. Browning trumpets

hang on the datura outside my window, the scent of sweetness tinged
　　　　with rot.
Or maybe you just don't love me enough.

I'm sorry I ate corned beef on rye at the 2nd Avenue Deli—
the cows crammed in factory feedlots.

And when I open the door for Elijah, I don't really want a stranger to enter.
I'm sorry I let the zucchinis grow too big. I'm sorry I planted zucchinis
　　　　altogether.

Forgive me, the sun will burn out.
I can't hear your heart beating in the silence between us.

The Kitchen Counter

Today I heard a young woman read a poem
in which her husband lifts her bare bottom
onto the kitchen counter
and, in the next line, spreads her legs.

The marriage has problems. They may already be divorced.
But suddenly I am ruing the fact
that no one has lifted my bottom onto a kitchen counter.

Not when my bottom trotted high and proud.
And not when it began to eye the floor
as if contemplating its future.

And now, I'm going to die
without ever being taken on those cold hard tiles.
Don't tell me it's not too late. It is.

Mammogram Callback with Ultrasound

So this is what I'm here for, to see inside
the mute weight of my right breast, heavy handful
of treasure I longed for as a girl, crying
behind the curtain in the Guerlain sisters' corset shop.
Those tender spinsters could hardly bear
my tears, as they adjusted the straps
on a padded lace bra. I had to wait another year
before my breasts swelled like wind-filled sails
and many were the explorers carried away,
searching for perfumes and spices,
the nerve-laden nipples singing through the wires.
But never has there been a joy like this
as I lie in the pale green cool of radiology.
The lineage of death has swerved around me.
More happy love! More happy, happy love!
As the wand of the ultrasound glides over my flesh,
revealed is a river of light, a bright
undulant tangle of lobules and milk ducts,
harmless and radiant against the black fat.
I could be looking up at the night sky,
this wispy band of brilliance
a shining spur of the Milky Way galaxy,
and I, in my infinitesimal life, will,
at least for tonight, keep these lovely atoms
before I must return them to the stars.

Blame

All around the cavernous room of the Cal Expo offtrack betting,
TVs blare simulcast as the crowd in jeans and sloppy sweatshirts
treks to the betting windows, trampling an autumn's worth of losing tickets.
The old man doesn't miss the emerald grass and red geraniums,
the women with big hats at Churchill Downs. He never tasted a mint julep
as the mahogany horses stepped out like carved statues.
And he doesn't mind the smell of stale beer or the damp cold
that seeps through his jacket and stiffens his already stiff hands.
He's spent weeks lying on his bed in the board and care
waiting for this moment when Zenyatta, the mare who never lost a race,
called in the *Times* "the coolest horse in the world,"
goes for twenty out of twenty. So the only question is who to place,
who to show, to make a trifecta that will bring back the days
when he skipped out on grinding afternoons at the dry cleaner's,
sweating at the mangle, saturated with solvent fumes,
as he bagged woolen coats and linen dresses and the jockeys' silks—
gleaming pinks, buttercup yellows, and aquamarines.
When they picked up their colors, they slipped him tips on who was hot,
and he'd escape to the track at Aqueduct to see those myths of muscle,
flanks quivering, flashing their tails. And now and then he'd score,
gather up the family and head to Chinatown for lobster with black bean sauce.
Once he even took them to Lancaster to see the Amish in their buggies,
their aprons and little white hats. But you could write the story
of all the paychecks fed like hay to the horses.
And he'll lose this one, too. In the final stretch,
Blame, a homebred chestnut colt in the lead.
Mike Smith up on Zenyatta closing hard, going to the whip.

Gopher

The pads of your paws scrabble
as I drag you from the tunnel
clamped to the shiny green trap,
a baby, hell-bent on saving
your twist of life, spun
from the same cells as I am, the common
intelligence of fins, wings, limbs.
The first time you see the sun
you're splayed on your back, the shadow
of my blade above you.
Your ears, tiny colorless petals,
and at the tips of your articulated fingers,
ten frantic claws. When I strike,
your mouth opens stunningly
wide, a scream so silent
all sound is sucked down the naked
whirlpool of your throat. I hate
that I can salvage nothing.
I can't skin and eat you, stuff or display
your fur on the mantel.
I won't carve a needle
from your bone. Bit of breath
I bury under a stone.

Because What We Do Does Not Die

This is not his face. This is not his breath.
This is a praise song
for the mother who sat down beside me,
her coat still on,
asking, *What is it, Ellen?*
This is homage to the mother
who hissed, *The bastard. The son of a bitch,*
I'm sorry you didn't bite his tongue off.
This is not his smell or the smell
of the grass he cut.
This is my mother the next day
in her clean blouse and crimson lipstick
waiting for him in the store,
quarts of clear vodka stacked behind her.
If you ever touch Ellen again, I'll tell your wife.
This is my mother pronouncing my name,
the name she crowned me.
If you see her on the street, cross
to the other side.
The man protested.
He needed the job. *I only kissed her.*
This is how I bow down to my mother,
my dead mother who will never be dead.
I never saw him again.
This is not his voice. This is not his tongue.

Marriage

When you finally, after long suffering, lay
the length of your body on mine, isn't it
like the strata of earth, the pressure
of time on sand, mud, bits of shell, the moving
water, wind, ice that carry the minutes,
minerals that fuse sediment into rock.
How to bear the weight, with every
flake of bone pressed in? O love,
it is balm and it seals. It binds us tight
as the fur of a rabbit to the rabbit.
When you strip it, grasping the edge
of the sliced skin, pulling the glossy membranes
apart, the body is warm and limp. If you could,
you'd climb inside that wet, slick skin
and carry it on your back. This is not
neat and white and lacy like a wedding,
not the bright effervescence of champagne
spilling over the throat of the bottle. This visceral
bloody union that is love, but
beyond love. Beyond charm and delight
the way you to yourself are past charm and delight.
This is the shucked meat of love, the alleys and broken
glass of love, the dizzy, hoarse cry, the stubborn hunger.

Pushing

This morning before we're even out of bed, she's
wading thigh deep in some kind of existential dread. She's been living
in a grotto of fear. Not suicidal—
her grandparents didn't flee the pogroms
just so she could down a handful of confetti-colored pills.
But she's asking why she is living
when every step she takes is a slog through this murky water.
Terrible as it is to admit, the first response I think of is
for a great cappuccino.
I'm remembering waking up in southern Italy
outside Alberobello. It was December and every day
we'd bundle up and walk into town to drink that creamy brew
with fresh-baked bread and slabs of butter.
But of course I don't say that.
I don't say anything.
I've already said every hopeful thing I can think of.
But she says, *I have to look at my fear with curiosity.*
Like when we were watching the larvae hatch.
A few weeks ago she found a cluster of eggs on a blackberry leaf.
When we got it under the hand lens,
they were glued together in a perfect symmetry.
And at that exact moment the first larvae were cracking
through their casings, white, soft-bodied babies pushing and pushing,
working to get through the tiny opening.
They'd swallowed the amniotic water and were swollen with it.
As I stared, scale shifted and the head of the one that was first
to be born began to seem huge as it labored toward release.
Like a human head trying to squeeze through the cervix.
We watched the slippery larva reach
the threshold and slide into the open,
bearing the command of its body to be born
and then to start eating the green flesh of the earth.
I remember how light she was, how almost happy,
and how, for a moment, I wasn't afraid.

Ode to Zeke

O breathing drum, O cask of dark
waters, O decaying star, my
barking heart, my breaking brother,
what will seep into the space
your body leaves? O huge
eighteen-muscled ears, oscillating
ossicles and cochlea, your busy canals
now hollow caves of quiet. I have said
your fur is black, but you are
silvered, rimed with frost.
You are the new moon.
You are light in the dark house.
How long will I see your shadow?
O heavy hunk of existence, O great flank
I have rested my head upon
when I was too weak for human touch.
Sleek leading man, you debonair dog,
how people on the avenue stopped to swoon.
O splaying legs once faster than rabbits,
canines slashing flesh. Urgent thug,
unstoppable thrust. O happy snapping
at the wind. What do you remember
now that you are mudslide, glacier
melting, cliff collapsing into the sea?
I have memorized your milky breath,
your ballet leaps and whirligigging.
Your princely patience, as the children
dressed you—Soccer Zeke
in jersey and shorts, one paw on the ball.
Snorkel Zeke with mask and fins.
Bar Mitzvah Zeke in a yarmulke
and my father's silk tallit. O my text
of decrepitude, my usher to death,

companion of ten thousand years,
I'll fry you a fish. I'll sit by your bowl.
Eat from my hand. I have nowhere to go.

Roses

Four roses drinking from a blue vase.
The first one I name Moment of Gladness,
the second, Wresting Beauty from Fear.
All year I watched her disappearing, the sweet fat
of her hips, her laughter, her will,
as though a whelk had drilled through her shell,
sucked out the flesh. Death woke me each morning
with its bird impersonation. But now she has cut
these Clouds of Glory and a honeyed musk sublimes
from their petals, veined fine as an infant's eyelids,
and spiraling like any embryo—fish, snake, or human.
And she has carried them to me, saturated
in the colors they have not swallowed,
the blush and gold, the razzle-dazzle red. Riven
from the dirt to cling here briefly.
And now, as though to signify our fortune,
a tiny insect journeys across the kingdom
of one ivory petal and into the heart
of the blossom. Oh, Small Mercies sliced
from the root. I listen
as they sip the blue water.

Kiss

When Lynne saw the lizard floating
in her mother-in-law's swimming pool,
she jumped in. And when it wasn't
breathing, its body limp as a baby
drunk on milk, she laid it on her palm
and pressed one fingertip to its silky breast
with just about the force you need
to test the ripeness of a peach, only quicker,
a brisk little push with a bit of spring in it.
Then she knelt, dripping wet in her Doc Martens
and camo T-shirt with the neck ripped out,
and bent her face to the lizard's face,
her big plush lips to the small stiff jaw
that she'd pried apart with her opposable thumb,
and she blew a tiny puff into the lizard's lungs.
The sun glared against the turquoise water.
What did it matter if she saved one lizard?
One lizard more or less in the world?
But she bestowed the kiss of life,
again and again, until
the lizard's wrinkled lids peeled back,
its muscles roused its own first breath
and she set it on the hot cement
where it rested a moment
before darting off.

After Long Illness

My wife calls. She left the eggs
she'd gathered in a small tin pail

and would I bring them in
so the dog doesn't eat them. Or maybe

he already has. They're by the shed
where we're trying to trap the rat

or maybe by the greenhouse.
I walk out in my robe and slippers, crushing

some mint which rewards me
with its sharp identity. And there

is the pail by the coop.
And there are two eggs, cold and whole

with a fleck of wood shaving stuck to one,
as though a child had just begun

to decorate it, maybe making a horse
with a tiny fetlock.

On My Father's Illness

My mother told me sometimes
she wished she could be like the other
wives, sit in the passenger seat,
pull down the little mirror in the visor
and put on her lipstick.

Photograph:
Jews Probably Arriving to the Lodz Ghetto circa 1941–1942

Why is a horse here
alongside the train? Two horses

yoked with leather harnesses, light
silvering their flanks

in the midst of the Jews
descending? Where is the driver

taking the cart, loaded
with wooden planks?

What is in the satchel
that weighs down the arm

of a woman in a dark coat,
her hair parted on one side?

A woman I could mistake
for my mother

in the family album. Only
my mother was in Philadelphia,

selling milk and eggs and penny candy
because her mother escaped the pogroms,

a small girl in steerage
crying for *her* mother.

What are the tight knots
of people saying to one another?

A star burns the right shoulder blade
of each man, each woman. Light strikes

What do you think?

BOOK TITLE: _____

COMMENTS: _____

_____

_____

OUR MISSION:

Poetry is vital to language and living. Copper Canyon Press publishes extraordinary poetry from around the world to engage the imaginations and intellects of readers.

Thank you for your thoughts!

Can we quote you? ☐ yes ☐ no

☐ Please send me a catalog full of poems and email news on forthcoming titles, readings, and poetry events.

☐ Please send me information on becoming a patron of Copper Canyon Press.

NAME: _____

ADDRESS: _____

CITY: _____ STATE: ____ ZIP: ____

EMAIL: _____

MAIL THIS CARD, SHARE YOUR COMMENTS ON FACEBOOK OR TWITTER,
OR EMAIL POETRY@COPPERCANYONPRESS.ORG

Copper Canyon Press

A nonprofit publisher dedicated to poetry

CopperCanyonPress.org

BUSINESS REPLY MAIL

FIRST-CLASS MAIL   PERMIT NO. 43   PORT TOWNSEND WA

POSTAGE WILL BE PAID BY ADDRESSEE

Copper Canyon Press
PO Box 271
Port Townsend, WA 98368-9931

each shorn neck
and caps each skull. No one is yet

stripped of all but a pail
or a tin to drink from and piss in.

Dread, like sun, sears the air
and breaks over the planes of their faces.

Light clatters down upon them
like stones, but we can't hear it.

Nor can we hear blood
thud under their ribs.

They will be led into the ghetto
and then will be led out to the camps,

but for now, the eternal now,
the light is silent,

silent the shadows
in the folds of their coats. The bones

of the horses are almost visible.
Their nostrils are deep, soft shadows.

And the woman,
who could be but is not

my mother,
still carries her canvas bag

and, looking closer,
what might be a small purse.

Pines at Ponary

One hundred thousand people were murdered by the
Nazis at Ponary, ten kilometers southwest of Vilnius,
where my grandmother was born.

Today is gray, drizzling,
but not enough for drops to pool
on the tips of the silver needles
or soak the bark of the pines at Ponary—
some of them more than a century old.
They were here when
the trains wheeled on numb
rails. And before I have gone
ten feet into the forest, I hear the sound.
Of course. There would have to be a train.
But I hadn't expected it still to run
like this, people
getting off and on with their packages.
I hadn't thought of the scent of resin spilling
into the cold afternoon. The trees
step to the rim
of the pits where Jews were shot
so the bodies fell in
efficiently. Their branches could save
no one. Their needles offered oxygen
to victims and executioners, the same.

Not Dead Yet

for Dan

The apricot tree with its amputated limbs
like a broken statue.

Condors. Bluefins. Lioness
at Amboseli, her bloodstained mouth.
She rises and walks beyond the shade of the thornbush,
crouches and pees.

My mother-in-law. Should I kill myself? she asks me—
her mind an abandoned building,
a few squatters lighting fires in the empty rooms.

Fire. Wildfires. The small animals running.

Paramecia swimming in a petri dish.

My son's rabbits nibbling grass. Soon
he'll cradle each one and speak to it
in a silent language
before breaking its neck. But today,
in the feverish heat, he wraps
his old T-shirt around a block of ice
for them to lean against.

Hair. Nails. Heart
carried in ice. Sperm
carried in a vial between a woman's breasts.

Bach. Coltrane. The ocean
even with its radiation and plastic islands.
Farmed salmon, even with their rotting flesh.

Two young women on the beach at Cala San Vicente.
One kisses the shoulder of the other
before she smooths on sunscreen.

Wind. The bougainvillea's shadow
shivering on the cold wall. Stone. The quiver
inside each atom.

Sappho: *mere air,*
these words, but delicious to hear.

I Could Touch It

When she was breaking apart, our son was falling in love.

She lay on the couch with a heated sack of rice on her belly,
sometimes dozing, sometimes staring out the window at the olive tree

as it broke into tiny white blossoms, as it swelled into bitter black fruit.

At first, I wanted to spare him.
I wished he was still farming up north, tucking bulbs of green onions
into their beds and watering the lettuce,
his hands gritty, his head haloed in a straw hat.

But as the months deepened, I grew selfish.

I wanted him here with his new love.
When I passed the open bathroom door, I wanted
to see them brushing their teeth,

one perched on the toilet lid, one on the side of the tub,
laughing and talking through their foamy mouths,
toothbrushes rattling against their teeth.

As sage gives its scent when you crush it. As stone
is hard. They were happy and I could touch it.

Ode to Fat

Tonight, as you undress, I watch your wondrous
flesh that's swelled again, the way a river swells
when the ice relents. Sweet relief
just to regard the sheaves of your hips,
your boundless breasts and marshy belly.
I adore the acreage
of your thighs and praise the promising
planets of your ass.
Oh, you were lean that terrifying year
you were unraveling, as though you were returning
to the slender scrap of a girl I fell in love with.
But your skin was vacant, a ripped sack,
sugar spilling out and your bones insistent.
Oh, praise the loyalty of the body
that labors to rebuild its palatial realm.
Bless butter. Bless brie.
Sanctify schmaltz. And cream and cashews.
Stoke the furnace
of the stomach and load the vessels. Darling,
drench yourself in opulent oil,
the lamp of your body glowing. May you always
flourish enormous and sumptuous,
be marbled with fat, a great vault that
I can enter, the cathedral where I pray.

Sometimes, when she is buried deep

between my thighs, rooted there
as a tree is rooted, digging into
my earth-heart, dirt-heart, heart riddled
with need and decay, breaking
down, breaking the world so
it can bud again, I become
the girl I was long ago, just out
of the gate, new to the track,
but with a will to run, my muscles
rippling like banners, my rump a blessing,
my scapulae wings. I'm so young
I smell like amniotic waters.
I squander my hot breath, careless
as wind whipping litter and fallen
leaves, rumbling empty cans, disturbing
any rest. How surprised I am to find myself
here again, at this cusp of crumbling,
this last dissolve, surrounded
by such succulent skin, and oh,
how she opens me, how she lifts me still.

Grizzly

She grazes in a meadow, sulfur blossoms spilling
from her jaw.

At this moment she seems so calm, she could be holy,
if what that means is something like being

wholly unaware of the good she gives,
how even her rooting tills the soil

and even her shitting ferries the seeds
and even her bathing is a joy to behold

as I am beholding her this morning
as she leans over a water hole, her shadow first

and then her reflection on the skin of the water,
then the splash as she enters, the pond opening,

rippling, and the scritch as she scrubs
her head with her paw, the great planet

of her head that she dunks and raises, shaking
the water in wide arcs, spraying

the lens of the hidden camera. And now
she climbs out, water rivering off her fur.

She is drying that huge head
in the long grasses.

And here she hunkers
over a bison carcass, slowly ripping free

the shoulder. Those precision instruments
that work with an ease that seems—yes—delicate.

Blood stains the river and stains
the snowbank and stains the rock.

Vessel carrying the chemicals of life—
hair and bone, flagella and bloom.

She carries them, lumbering forward
as she sinks her teeth and feeds.

Sink Your Fingers into the Darkness of My Fur

Until this sore minute, you could turn the key, pivot away.

But mine is the only medicine now

wherever you go or follow.

The past is so far away, but it flickers,

then cleaves the night. The bones

of the past splinter between our teeth.

This is our life, love. Why did I think

it would be anything less than too much

of everything? I know you remember that cheap motel

on the coast where we drank red wine,

the sea flashing its gold scales as sun

soaked our skin. You said, This must be

what people mean when they say

I could die now. Now

we're so much closer

to death than we were then. Who isn't crushed,

stubbed out beneath a clumsy heel?

Who hasn't stood at the open window,

sleepless, for the solace of the damp air?

I had to get old to carry both buckets

yoked on my shoulders. Sweet

and bitter waters I drink from.

Let me know you, ox you.

I want your scent in my hair.

I want your jokes.

Hang your kisses on all my branches, please.

Sink your fingers into the darkness of my fur.

The title is taken from Olli Heikkonen's poem of the same title, translated from Finnish by Maria Lyytinen.

Fungus on Fallen Alder at Lookout Creek

Florid, fluted, flowery petal, flounce
of a girl's dress, ruffled fan,
striped in what seems to my simple eye
an excess of extravagance,
intricately ribboned like a secret
code, a colorist's vision of DNA.
At the outermost edge a scallop
of ivory, then a tweedy russet,
then mouse gray, a crescent
of celadon velvet, a streak of sleek seal brown,
a dark arc of copper, then butter,
then celadon again, again butter, again
copper and on into the center, striped thinner
and thinner to the green, green moss-furry heart.
How can this be necessary?
Yet it grows and is making more
of itself, dozens and dozens of tiny starts, stars
no bigger than a baby's thumbnail,
all of them sucking one young dead tree
on a gravel bank that will be washed away
in the next flooding winter. But isn't the air here
cool and wet and almost unbearably sweet?

I look over and there she is

reading on the couch, her messy hair
finally beginning to gray. She is
breathing, moving molecules
of air aside, inhabiting
space that could go empty
so easily. She holds
a heating pad to her side
where I bruised her rib, clumsy
in my hunger for her infinite
variety. *Ya'aburnee,*
lovers say in Arabic—
you bury me.
It's quiet enough
that I can hear the ringing always
in the background now. A page rustles
as she turns it. Ice
melting in my glass topples
with a little clink.

This Was the Door

There was no beauty
when I sat at the kitchen table, breaking

open the pinkish capsules, dividing the granules
so she could swallow the precise promise,

where she lay in the backyard wrapped in quilts
every night staring up through the branches, stars

flecked in the black-veined sky.
There was no time

out there. Or time was large enough to hold her.
One moon slowly rolling over. I waited

long as I could. Then we began.
A bath. Tea. Litanies

of consolation, though she was inconsolable.
I rubbed her feet before the door

which led to a sleepless night or
to the night of us split

into the cells of our separate dreams. Through the window,
the patience of trees.

I was so tired. I told myself she wasn't dead.
She wasn't dying. I called it the hellhole.

It's only with distance
we can bear the beauty

of that much burning, the light
having traveled so long, so far.

Ever-Changing Song

First a spout
bursting through

all that blue with the sun clanging on it,
then a slope,

wheeling, almost slowly,
through the blue air, and four times—

or maybe five—I see her dive,
the dark flukes flaring,

silhouetted, raised heavy for a moment into all that light.
If I paddled a canoe or could swim that far, we might meet,

her great eye opening to my small one, each cornea
bending the light,

setting off the translation into vision, gazing
into the dark pupil of the other.

Indigo

As I'm walking on West Cliff Drive, a man runs
toward me pushing one of those jogging strollers
with shock absorbers so the baby can keep sleeping,
which this baby is. I can just get a glimpse
of its almost translucent eyelids. The father is young,
a jungle of indigo and carnelian tattooed
from knuckle to jaw, leafy vines and blossoms,
saints and symbols. Thick wooden plugs pierce
his lobes and his sunglasses testify
to the radiance haloed around him. I'm so jealous.
As I often am. It's a kind of obsession.
I want him to have been my child's father.
I want to have married a man who wanted
to be in a body, who wanted to live in it so much
that he marked it up like a book, underlining,
highlighting, writing in the margins, I was *here*.
Not like my dead ex-husband, who was always
fighting against the flesh, who sat for hours
on his zafu chanting *om* and then went out
and broke his hand punching the car.
I imagine when this galloping man gets home
he's going to want to have sex with his wife,
who slept in late, and then he'll eat
barbecued ribs and let the baby teethe on a bone
while he drinks a dark beer. I can't stop
wishing my daughter had had a father like that.
I can't stop wishing I'd had that life. Oh, I know
it's a miracle to have a life. Any life at all.
It took eight years for my parents to conceive me.
First there was the war and then just waiting.
And my mother's bones so narrow, she had to be slit
and I airlifted. That anyone is born,
each precarious success from sperm and egg
to zygote, embryo, infant, is a wonder.

And here I am, alive.
Almost seventy years and nothing has killed me.
Not the car I totaled running a stop sign
or the spirochete that screwed into my blood.
Not the tree that fell in the forest exactly
where I was standing—my best friend shoving me
backward so I fell on my ass as it crashed.
I'm alive.
And I gave birth to a child.
So she didn't get a father who'd sling her
onto his shoulder. And so much else she didn't get.
I've cried most of my life over that.
And now there's everything that we can't talk about.
We love—but cannot take
too much of each other.
Yet she is the one who, when I asked her to kill me
if I no longer had my mind—
we were on our way into Ross,
shopping for dresses. That's something
she likes and they all look adorable on her—
she's the only one
who didn't hesitate or refuse
or waver or flinch.
As we strode across the parking lot
she said, OK, but when's the cutoff?
That's what I need to know.

Any Common Desolation

can be enough to make you look up
at the yellowed leaves of the apple tree, the few
that survived the rains and frost, shot
with late afternoon sun. They glow a deep
orange-gold against a blue so sheer, a single bird
would rip it like silk. You may have to break
your heart, but it isn't nothing
to know even one moment alive. The sound
of an oar in an oarlock or a ruminant
animal tearing grass. The smell of grated ginger.
The ruby neon of the liquor store sign.
Warm socks. You remember your mother,
her precision a ceremony, as she gathered
the white cotton, slipped it over your toes,
drew up the heel, turned the cuff. A breath
can uncoil as you walk across your own muddy yard,
the Big Dipper pouring night down over you, and everything
you dread, all you can't bear, dissolves
and, like a needle slipped into your vein—
that sudden rush of the world.

About the Author

Ellen Bass has published several award-winning books of poetry, including *Like a Beggar, The Human Line,* and *Mules of Love.* Her poems have frequently appeared in *The New Yorker, The American Poetry Review,* and many other journals. She coedited the groundbreaking anthology of women's poetry *No More Masks!,* and her nonfiction includes the best-selling *The Courage to Heal.* Among her awards are fellowships from the National Endowment for the Arts and the California Arts Council, three Pushcart prizes, and the Lambda Literary Award. A chancellor of the Academy of American Poets, she teaches in the MFA writing program at Pacific University.

The book you are holding is a testament to the diverse community of passionate readers who supported "Indigo: New Poetry by Ellen Bass." Copper Canyon Press is deeply grateful to the following individuals around the world whose philanthropic vision and love of poetry made this collection possible. We have published *Indigo* together. Thank you!

Anonymous
Ginney Agnew
Kelli Russell Agodon
Susan Alexander
Mary Jo Amani
Carrie Anders
Claressinka Anderson
Loretta Libby Atkins
Eloise Ruth Auld
Michelle M. Ballou
David Alexander Beame
Donna Bellew
Twanna P. Bolling
Michele Bombardier
Partridge Boswell
Richard A. Brait
Lisa Brown
Louise Brown
Shirley Buccieri
Vincent & Jane Buck
Joanna Candler
Sarah & Tim Cavanaugh
Tina Cervin
Victoria Chang
In memory of Catherine
   M. Clem
Graham Coppin
David Curry
Lila Danielle
Pam Davenport
Pamela Davis
David de Weese
Jill Deasy
Kathryn Dunlap
Jay Edwards & Mason
   Funk
Jane W. Ellis
Tyler Erlendson
Sigrid Erro

Jenny Factor
Tyra Ferlatte
Iyla Wren Fox
Constance Frenzen
Alison G.
Gary Gangnes
Loretta Gase
Linda Gerrard
Jeanne Glad
Kip Greenthal
Anne Griffin
Dick Guthrie
Cecelia Hagen
In memory of Jim
   Harrison
In honor of Mary Heffron
In honor of Florence
   Howe
Susan Johnston
Kathryn Jordan
Victoria Kaplan
In honor of Shirley Klock
   and Sam
George Knotek
KZ
Jim Lenfestey
Ann Maioroff
Jessica Manack
Susan Maresco
Brian Marsh
In memory of T. Craig
   Martin
Larry Mawby
Ivana Mestrovic
D. Miller
Patti Klumpp Miller
Joseph P. Morra
Joan L Murphy
Elaine A. Nelson

In memory of poet Sharon
   H. Nelson
Kim Noriega
Anne O'Donnell
Resnick Ohana
Patricia Percival
Kimberley Pittman-Schulz
Linda Plutynski
Michael A. Ponsor
Jory Post
Anne Pound
Sophie Raymond
Barb Reynolds
In honor of E. LaRae
   Rhoads
Stuart Rickey
Sara Ritter
Richard L. Rose
Richard Rozen
Pamela J. Sampel
Kim & Jeff Seely
Dory Sheldon
Zia Shepherd
Rick Simonson
Pamela Sinicrope
Maggie Slocumb
Katherine Olivia Soniat
Kate Sontag
Raymond & Nancy
   Steinberg
Susan Thom
Dawn Tripp
Rolland Vasin
Dee Vogel & Lin Marelick
Connie Wieneke
Katherine Williams
Christy Wise
Paul Woodruff

Poetry is vital to language and living. Since 1972, Copper Canyon Press has published extraordinary poetry from around the world to engage the imaginations and intellects of readers, writers, booksellers, librarians, teachers, students, and donors.

IN MEMORY AND DEEP APPRECIATION OF LINDA GERRARD FOR HER PASSIONATE LOVE OF POETRY AND FAITHFUL SUPPORT OF COPPER CANYON PRESS

WE ARE GRATEFUL FOR THE MAJOR SUPPORT PROVIDED BY:

THE PAUL G. ALLEN FAMILY FOUNDATION

Anonymous

Jill Baker and Jeffrey Bishop

Anne and Geoffrey Barker

Donna and Matthew Bellew

Diana Broze

John R. Cahill

The Beatrice R. and Joseph A. Coleman Foundation Inc.

The Currie Family Fund

Laurie and Oskar Eustis

Saramel and Austin Evans

Mimi Gardner Gates

Gull Industries Inc. on behalf of William True

The Trust of Warren A. Gummow

Carolyn and Robert Hedin

Phil Kovacevich and Eric Wechsler

Lakeside Industries Inc. on behalf of Jeanne Marie Lee

Maureen Lee and Mark Busto

Peter Lewis

Ellie Mathews and Carl Youngmann as The North Press

Larry Mawby

Hank Meijer

Jack Nicholson

Petunia Charitable Fund and adviser Elizabeth Hebert

Gay Phinny

Suzie Rapp and Mark Hamilton

Adam and Lynn Rauch

Emily and Dan Raymond

Jill and Bill Ruckelshaus

Cynthia Sears

Kim and Jeff Seely

Dan Waggoner

Randy and Joanie Woods

Barbara and Charles Wright

Caleb Young as C. Young Creative

The dedicated interns and faithful volunteers of Copper Canyon Press

The Chinese character for poetry is made up of two parts:
"word" and "temple."
It also serves as pressmark for Copper Canyon Press.

This book is set in Estilo and Scala.
Design by Katy Homans.
Printed on archival-quality paper.